Portishead

Past and Present

by
Kenneth Crowhurst
A collection of photographs of old Portishead with present day comparisons
Present day photographs by author

European Library – Zaltbommel/Netherlands

Acknowledgements:
I would like to thank the following people who have allowed me to reproduce photographs from their collections: Mrs. P.M. Bishop, Bristol City Museum, Mr. M. Bye, Mr. R. Bye, Mr. G. Coles, County of Avon (Portishead Library), Miss W. Harris, Mrs. D. Mapstone, Mr. K. Selvey and Mr. M.J. Tozer.

About the author:
Kenneth Crowhurst was born at Tilbury, Essex, and was educated at Palmer's School at Grays, Essex. He first lived in the West country when he was evacuated to a farm in Wilthsire in 1940, but did not settle permanently in the West until he moved to Portishead in 1970 through his employment as an accountant in the Civil Service. His interest in photography led him to collecting local postcards and old views of Portishead, and he is a member of the Local History Group of the Gordano Society.

By the same author:
Portishead in old picture postcards (European Library, 1987).

GB   ISBN 90 288 4703 0 / CIP

© 1988 European Library – Zaltbommel/Netherlands

Portishead

INTRODUCTION

Being a keen photographer and having access to many old views of Portishead, both from my own collection and from friends who share my interest in local history, I felt that it would be a useful contribution to local knowledge to make a photographic record of the town in 1988. By means of a series of comparable past and present views, this book shows how much or how little the local scene has changed over the last century.

During the last few months, I have explored many parts of Portishead new to me in the course of this project, and have had many interesting conversations with local people in my quest to discover the viewpoints from which the 'past' photographs were taken. In a number of cases, I have found it quite impossible to re-photograph the old views exactly, because new developments have blocked them out, but from a total of some eighty pairs of views I have chosen a representative selection which takes the reader on a tour of Portishead, starting in the area of St. Peter's Church. The route follows the High Street past the docks along to the pier, then round to Battery Point and past the Lake Grounds to Nore Road and along to Redcliffe Bay, ending up on Down Road.

The oldest views in the book are of the High Street area, taken almost a century ago, and show Portishead at that time to have been a relatively quiet backwater of North Somerset, just beginning to enjoy the new prosperity brought to the village by the coming of the railway in 1867 and by the opening of the dock in 1879. Much of Portishead was owned, and still is, by Bristol Corporation who were largely responsible for its development during the nineteenth century as a seaside resort, as a residential village for Bristol businessmen wishing to live outside the City and as an industrial centre.

I feel that these contrasted photographs tell their own story of the process of change in the appearance of Portishead during the last hundred years. The pace of change has been particularly rapid during the last twenty-five years and has brought with it an ever-increasing traffic problem. Both residents and visitors obviously consider it to be an attractive spot – let us hope that future expansion is kept to the minimum in order to avoid spoiling the environment which people now enjoy.

Kenneth Crowhurst

30065 Portishead. General View.

1. *General view from Fore Hill – c. 1910.* The houses at the left foreground are on Newlands Hill and Quarry Lane leads across to the right. There are extensive orchards in the centre of the view, lying between Slade Road and the High Street, and in the distance lies the dock with Woodhill to the left.

General view from Fore Hill – 1988. The town centre is now filled with housing and the orchards have gone. Quarry Lane now has houses along it and St. Peter's churchyard is considerably larger. One of Albright and Wilson's ships is in the dock and to its left is the now decommissioned Portishead 'B' Power Station awaiting demolition.

Interior Parish Church Portishead.

2. *Interior of St. Peter's Parish Church – c. 1915.* This card was posted in 1915 and shows the oak screen erected in 1910 across the chancel arch in place of the previous wrought iron screen. The font in the foreground was a replacement for the old Norman font thrown out during the 19th century.

Interior of St. Peter's Parish Church – 1988. The oak screen has gone and the carved pews were replaced by chairs during the 1970s. The font in the previous view has been taken out and the old Norman font has been restored to the church – it now stands at the west end of the north aisle.

3. *Corner of High Street and Albert Road – c. 1950.* This corner was occupied by the *Victoria Inn* from the turn of the century until it was demolished along with a number of other adjoining properties in the late 1960s. *(Mrs. D. Mapstone)*

Corner of High Street and Albert Road – 1988. After the demolitions of the 1960s, Victoria Square stood derelict, used only for car parking, for over ten years until the sheltered housing known as Victoria Court was erected on the site in 1982.

4. *Old Cottage, High Street – c. 1906.* For many years during the nineteenth century, this was the home and business premises of Stephen Tuck, proprietor of various horse-drawn transport such as omnibuses, flys, cabs and carriages. He also operated a thrice-weekly carriage service from Portishead to Bristol.

Post Office, High Street – 1988. The old thatched cottage was demolished in the 1930s to provide a site for Portishead's new Post Office. The Bristol & West building was previously used by the National Westminster Bank until it moved to its present site further along the High Street in the mid-1970s.

5. *High Street scene – c. 1914.* What an unusual sight this must have been for the villagers when this advertising cart drawn by four zebras and attended by three Ceylonese appeared in the High Street to promote Mazawattee – 'A blend specially flavoured with tea from the sweet scented island Ceylon which produces the most luscious tea in the world.' The shop behind was the grocery run by the Harris family – Mr. Huntley Harris can be seen behind the zebras wearing a straw boater, and his daughter Winifred is sitting on one of the zebras. Beside her is the man organising the promotion. *(Miss W.M. Harris)*

High Street scene – 1988. The former grocery store is now Freemans TV and video shop and the railings and garden have been replaced by a garage and service station. The only zebras in the High Street today are the pedestrian crossings!

6. *High Street – c. 1920.* The High Street scene outside the Post Office on the right seems fairly busy and appears to be a popular meeting spot for the local lads – one in the background has a handcart and is probably a delivery boy. Horsepower and bicycles still seem to be the principal methods of local travel.

High Street – 1988. The road has been widened at the expense of the properties on the left, and it is no longer safe to stand and chat in the middle of the road. Shop fronts have changed but apart from the new shop run by Gateway, most of the buildings look the same so far as the rooflines are concerned.

7. *Thomas Coles's Office – c. 1924.* Thomas Coles (left) stands beside a model 'T' Ford parked outside the Central Motor Garage in the High Street – his son George is on the right. He started his business as a daily carrier to Bristol using a horse-drawn covered wagon in 1896, but by the time this photograph was taken he was using a motor van, as advertised on his board. He also installed the first petrol pump in Portishead in the front garden of his office – the pump in the picture bears the words 'Filtered Petrol'. *(Mr. G. Coles)*

Catherine's Patisserie – 1988. Even though the premises are now a patisserie, the old house shows little change upstairs and the back yard is still in the transport business – today it offers car repairs and taxis. The old cottages which stood to the left and right of this house were demolished and the sites have been redeveloped with shops and flats.

High Street, Portishead

8. *High Street – c. 1910.* This was virtually a 'pedestrian precinct' when this view was taken – there was not a lot of danger for children using the High Street as a playground in those days! On the right was Bowen's, stationer and stockist of fancy goods, and further along was Clark's Grocery, next door to the arched façade of the National Provincial Bank.

High Street – 1988. Shops have changed hands many times during the intervening years and shop fronts have been altered but the general outline of the High Street shows relatively little change.

9. *High Street – c. 1909*. This card was posted in 1909 and shows a small group standing outside The Central Shaving Salon run by Mr. Fred Smith (right), holding his eldest son Fred. In the centre with his dog is Capt. Hawkes and on the left Mr. John Broome. Jameson's jewellers shop is to the left. The Salon's advertisements include several brands of tobacco long since gone – Kentucky Mixture, Rajah Cigars and Exmoor Hunt Mixture.

High Street – 1988. Central House has acquired a non-matching extension on its right-hand end, but it is interesting to see that the original ornamented doorways and stone window surrounds still remain – most of the other old shop fronts in the High Street have been 'modernised' in the name of progress.

10. *High Street – c. 1890.* With six horse-drawn carts in the High Street all at the same time, this old view must have been taken in the rush hour! The boy is riding a most unusual tricycle – it could almost be described as a twopence-farthing! *(Bristol City Museum and Art Gallery)*

High Street – 1988. When compared with the previous view, the only new buildings visible in this photograph are those in the far distance which were built around 1902-3. They were constructed on the site of the old cottages that can be seen in the previous view.

11. *High Street – c. 1890*. The left-hand end of this building was known as Neville House and was at that time occupied by Mr. S. Small, carpenter, builder and undertaker. He was also agent for Challicoms of Clevedon who operated vans for furniture removals to all parts by road or rail. In the centre was Mr. Alexander Dawes, assistant overseer, who describes himself as auctioneer & valuer and estate & house agent. The right-hand end of the building was known as Rembrandt House and was the business premises of Mr. William Wade & Son, plumber, glazier, painter and paperhanger. His shop window is full of oil lamps of every description and he has advertisements for Sunlight Soap and Wade's Pure Oils. *(Mrs. P.M. Bishop)*

High Street – 1988. Today there are only two separate business premises in this building, the Midland Bank occupying both the left-hand and central shops. The name Rembrandt House is still visible over the side door to the right-hand shop, but at the time this photograph was taken the shop was vacant.

12. *British Legion Hut – c. 1935*. Taken from the top of the wall in front of the Methodist Church, this photograph is of a Remembrance Day Parade in front of the British Legion hut which stood on ground adjacent to the White Lion. The High Street at that time continued along towards Station Road, bounded by a stone wall on the far side. The land on which the hut stood was owned by the Great Western Railway, whose notice advertises 'Frontage Building Plots to Let on a Ninety Nine Years' Lease'. *(Mr. R. Bye)*

High Street/Wyndham Way junction – 1988. Today's view from the same point looks across an entirely different scene, and it is no longer possible to see across to the docks due to the growth of Portishead's light industrial estate.

Woodhill from Railway Station, Portishead

13. *Woodhill from the Railway Station – c. 1908.* This was the view from the terminus of the Weston, Clevedon & Portishead Light Railway, which stood about a hundred yards behind the White Lion, looking towards Woodhill – to the right are the waters of the pill before the ground was in-filled. The large building on the extreme left stands at the corner of Cabstand and Station Road.

Wyndham Way – 1988. Today's view is dominated by the Esso filling station which blocks off the former view of Woodhill. Station Ford's car showroom is part of the booking hall of Portishead's new British Railway station which came into service in 1954 as a replacement for the former station demolished to make way for Portishead 'B' Power Station. This new station in its turn fell victim to the Beeching axe in 1964.

Weston and Clevedon Light Railway Terminus, Portishead

14. *Weston and Clevedon Light Railway Terminus, Portishead – c. 1913.* The Weston & Clevedon Light Railway was extended to Portishead in 1907 and terminated at this simple timber building which contained a waiting room, booking office and a ladies' room. It was reached by a lane from the High Street which ran underneath an archway, still visible today, in the White Lion. A number of horse-drawn carriages or flys can be seen setting down or picking up passengers on this postcard which was posted in 1913.

Wyndham Way – 1988. From the rear of the Somerset Hall, on the right of this view, to the point in the distance where the road crosses the main drainage rhyne for the valley, Wyndham Way follows the former track bed of the W.C. & P.L.R. The line ceased operation in 1940 and the new road into Portishead was opened in the early 1970s.

15. *T. Coles's Garage, Cabstand – c. 1919.* In addition to his premises shown at No. 7, Mr. Thomas Coles had a garage at the bottom of Cabstand from which char-à-banc excursions were operated for day trippers to places such as Weston super Mare and Cheddar Gorge. Mr. Coles can be seen standing in the gateway and his son George is fifth from the right, wearing a straw boater. In the yard behind is the same model 'T' Ford seen in the photograph at No. 7. *(Mr. G. Coles)*

Station Ford, Cabstand – 1988. This property with a garage to the rear was built by Mr. T. Coles in 1927 as his Cabstand business premises. It is now used by Station Ford for its offices and parts department, and the garage behind is still in use as a workshop.

16. *New Union Chapel and Woodhill Road – c. 1900.* When this photograph was taken, the gate across Woodhill Road was still in place – tolls were paid to the tollkeeper who lived in the gatehouse which dates back to 1828, the time when Bristol Corporation began spending money on Portishead to improve its attractions as a watering place within easy reach of Bristol. The New Union Chapel was built in the incredibly short space of fifteen months and the first service was held there in 1877. *(Mr. M. Bye)*

United Reformed Church and Woodhill Road – 1988. Apart from the painting of the lines on the road, and the removal of the gates and some trees in Woodhill Road, this scene has hardly changed for ninety years. The Union Chapel subsequently became known as the Union Congregational Church, but is now the United Reformed Church.

17. *Battery Road – c. 1900.* Taken not long after they were built by local builder Mr. George Biss, this view shows Cambrian Lodge and Fairlawns in Battery Road next to the New Union Chapel. Land to the left of Cambrian Lodge was originally occupied by its stables. *(Mrs. P.M. Bishop)*

Battery Road – 1988. Cambrian Lodge and Fairlawns have almost disappeared behind the front garden trees and both are now residential homes. Cambrian Lodge has been extended and re-roofed but has unfortunately lost its beautifully carved barge boards and decorative timber-work. Its stables were demolished and replaced by a bungalow, but this in turn has been taken down and replaced by an obtrusive development of flats.

18. *Parish wharf – c. 1910.* Before the coming of the railway in the 1860s and the docks in the 1870s, Portishead pill was open to the tides of the Bristol Channel which brought the waters up to the White Lion and to the Parish wharf opposite. Under the terms of the 1866 Portishead Pier & Railway Act, the two roods of land originally occupied by the Parish wharf were exchanged for half an acre of land with a landing stage on the south-west side of the pill, close to the new railway line. This postcard shows coal being loaded on to a cart at the wharf. The steamships on the right are alongside the timber wharf. *(County of Avon – Portishead Library)*

Parish wharf – 1988. Cargoes are no longer unloaded at the Parish wharf, but it is nowadays used for pleasure purposes by the Portishead Cruising Club. The ship on the right is the 'Albright Explorer', unloading phosphorous at Albright and Wilson's plant, while on the left the huge edifice of Portishead 'B' Power Station awaits demolition.

At the Pier, Portishead

19. *At the pier – c. 1905.* A small group of people are standing at the top of the steps leading down to the pier watching the shipping in King Road on a calm day. The largest ship is the Bristol Training Ship H.M.S. '*Formidable*' aboard which were trained more than 3,500 poor and destitute boys between 1869 and 1906. To the right of the '*Formidable*' is its tender '*Polly*', a brigantine of approximately 125 tons, used to send thirty boys at a time on training cruises. In 1897, '*Polly*' was present at Queen Victoria's Diamond Jubilee Review at Spithead – the yards were manned and a Royal salute was blown by bugler Biggs as the Royal Yacht proceeded down the lines.

At the pier – 1988. There is very little shipping for people to stand and watch today and the pier is only used on the occasions of the infrequent visits during the summer season of the '*Balmoral*' or the P.S. '*Waverley*'. The former wooden pier has been replaced by one constructed in concrete.

Royal Hotel, Portishead

20. *Royal Hotel – c. 1910.* A view of the Royal Hotel, built in 1830, from the pier.

Royal Hotel – 1988. The only difference between this view and the previous one is the disappearance of the 'Royal Hotel' sign – from this point of view, it all looks very much the same.

21. *Esplanade from Battery Point – 1938.* Looking across the miniature golf course and Woodhill Bay, the masts of Portishead Radio Station can be seen on the top of Portishead Down.

Swimming Pool and Esplanade – 1988. The open-air swimming pool was constructed in 1962 on the site of the miniature golf course. The mud-flats are now covered with marram grass, and houses built during the last twenty years cover the north-facing upper slopes of the Down. The service provided by the Radio Station was transferred to Burnham-on-Sea in 1978 and the masts were taken down the following year. The name lives on, however, as the station at Burnham is still known worldwide as Portishead Radio Station.

37408   THE MARINE LAKE AND BAY, PORTISHEAD.

22. *Marine Lake and Bay – c. 1938.* This view looks across the grass courts of the tennis club to the Marine Lake and Esplanade on which stands the shelter facing the Lake Grounds known locally as the 'beehive'. Lake Road crosses the foreground.

Marine Lake and Bay – 1988. Today the tennis club has hard courts and a new club house, and the previously uncultivated area to the right is now the miniature golf course. The 'beehive' has been demolished and has been replaced by two modern style shelters; the Marine Lake has acquired a new larger boathouse.

23. *Rodmoor – c. 1895.* Rodmoor was the most northerly of the Somerset levels and was for centuries a natural marshland teeming with wildlife and marsh birds such as snipe. With the growth of Portishead's population during the 19th century it was drained sufficiently to permit its use as a pasture – this photograph shows signs of drainage channels and there are some cows grazing; two haystacks can be seen in the field behind the cattle. *(Mrs. P.M. Bishop)*

Marine Lake – 1988. Part of Rodmoor was dug out by hand in 1910 to form a Marine Lake as part of the Bristol Corporation's plan to improve the amenities and attractions of Portishead and at the same time to provide work for some of Bristol's unemployed who were brought in each day by train from Ashton Gate. This view was taken on a mid-week evening with few people around – quite different from the weekends when the Lake Grounds prove very popular with visitors.

24. *Lake Grounds – c. 1915.* This well-dressed group of young ladies, probably in their Sunday best, are no doubt wishing that they too could be taken for a row on the Marine Lake.

Lake Grounds – 1988. This was taken on a sunny Sunday afternoon when the Lake Grounds were busy with visitors, young and old, relaxing and enjoying themselves – the boats are still as popular as they were when the Marine Lake was first opened.

The AVENUE BEACH ROAD Portishead 417

25. *The Avenue, Beach Road – c. 1917.* A local baker's cart is making deliveries along this shady avenue of trees; they were planted around the turn of the century when Beach Road was extended to meet Battery Road.

Beach Road – 1988. The trees along the right-hand side of the road have gone, but the row on the left is largely intact. Bungalows have been built along the right side of Beach Road with a fine view overlooking the lake. The houses along Rodmoor Road in the middle distance on the left were built during the 1930s.

WOODHILL FROM NORE ROAD, PORTISHEAD. 25

26. *Woodhill from Nore Road – c. 1910.* This small triangular island with its elegant street lamp acquired the nickname of Lorrimer's 'Park' or 'Piece' after Mr. J. Lorrimer, Chairman of Portishead Urban District Council from 1898 to 1901. It was surrounded by iron railings with a chain along the top, and had a seat for local people to sit and enjoy the view of the Point. When Eric Wright took this photograph, the 'Park' visitors included a lady in a bathchair and a child in a perambulator. *(M.J. Tozer)*

Woodhill from Nore Road – 1988. The 'Park' minus its railings is still in position and still has a seat, but with its modern street furniture it looks somewhat less elegant than it did previously; the old cottages beyond it have been replaced. During the Second World War it must have been regarded as a very strategic location because it was selected as the site for a pillbox!

27. *Battery Point from Nore Road – c. 1895.* Only a bank of stones and shingle prevented the high tides from flooding low-lying Rodmoor when this photograph was taken, because the Esplanade was not constructed until 1898; the house visible on Battery Point was reputedly occupied by the caretaker of the fort. Of the three houses along Beach Road, the one in the middle is the oldest, dating from about 1832. *(Mrs. P.M. Bishop)*

Battery Point from Nore Road – 1988. The previously cultivated field is now used for leisure purposes and a seat has been provided for people to sit and watch the shipping or the glorious summer sunsets across the Channel. Housing along Battery Lane and Lake Road has encroached upon the old pasture lands and the concrete of the open-air swimming pool dominates the Point.

28. *Nore Road – c. 1905.* A peaceful scene with a pony and trap emerging from the thickly wooded stretch of Nore Road.

Nore Road – 1988. The road is now wider and only a few elms of the former avenue remain, most having been felled for safety reasons. On the left are the houses of Mariners Park, built in the early 1970s, and on the right is the Approach Golf Course.

GOLF LINKS, PORTISHEAD. Nº 2

29. *Golf Club House – c. 1910.* This view from Nore Road, looking across the Channel, shows the Golf Club House built in 1908 incorporating the disused tower of Portishead windmill which dates from 1832. The golf course was a full eighteen holes, above and below Nore Road, and was designed by Harry Vardon, six times winner of the British Open and also winner of the U.S. Open.

Hole in One – 1988. Now the '*Hole in One*', the former Golf Club House is now a public house and restaurant. It still looks very much the same, and customers get a good view of the shipping and local yacht club activities.

45375   NORE ROAD AND GENERAL VIEW, PORTISHEAD.

30. *Nore Road and General View – c. 1950.* The golf course was ploughed up during the last war as part of the effort to grow more food, but was not restored to its previous use after 1945. When this photograph was taken, it was simply a grassy hillside. In the distance, on the right, are the two chimneys of Portishead 'A' Power Station – the 'B' Station was not built until the mid-1950s.

Mariners Park Estate – 1988. The land was sold for development in the 1960s and building has continued spasmodically on the Estate over the last twenty years. In contrast to the previous view, the two Power Station chimneys visible belong to Portishead 'B' Station, the 'A' Station having been demolished in 1981.

THE NORE RD PORTISHEAD.

31. *Nore Road – c. 1900.* The message on this card reads: 'A lovely place – indeed it is rather becoming known as the Riviera of England. The woods abound, and also the roads about the place are beautiful.' Between Nore Road and the Channel can be seen the tower of the disused windmill with Windmill Cottage to its left.

Nore Road – 1988. The present day road is wider, with a footpath, and most of the trees have gone. The old windmill tower has been incorporated into the '*Hole in One*', and the former grazing land on the left is now occupied by the Approach Golf Course.

32488   BATHING BEACH AND CHILDREN'S POOL. PORTISHEAD

32. *Bathing Beach and Children's Pool – 1940s.* The Loaf Bathing Beach was one of Portishead's most popular spots and boasted a café, changing cubicles and a children's paddling pool refilled at each tide. The 'Loaf' rock at the far end of the beach was used for diving and had an iron ladder and a diving board fixed to it.

Loaf Beach – 1988. This photograph was taken on a Sunday afternoon but there was not a bather in sight. The main users these days are the members of Portishead Yacht and Sailing Club who have their headquarters here and launch their yachts from the beach.

33. *Glenwood Café, Nore Road – c. 1932.* The Glenwood Café with its distinctive Thirties' styling and situated in very rural surroundings was a popular place for teas and refreshments.

What's in Store, Nore Road – 1988. The lane by the side of the former café is now Glenwood Rise. The building has housed a variety of businesses during its lifetime and is currently a store and Off-licence.

Nore Road, Redcliffe Bay, Portishead.

34. *Nore Road, Redcliffe Bay – c. 1933*. With the development of Redcliffe Bay during the 1920s, Nore Road was gradually extended and improved as this card posted in 1933 shows; the turning to the left is Newhaven Place.

Nore Road, Redcliffe Bay – 1988. The timber and asbestos bungalows across the road have been demolished and Hillcrest Road now joins Nore Road at this point. Power lines with their supporting poles tend to spoil today's views.

Pathway to Bungalows, Redcliffe Bay, Portishead

35. *Pathway to Bungalows, Redcliffe Bay – c. 1933.* From the lane beside the Channel a narrow pathway leads up to the bungalows, each of which stands in a generously-sized plot.

Junction of Heavens Lane and Hillside Road – 1988. The former pathway is now Heavens Lane, wide enough to take cars, and the coastal lane has become Hillside Road. The portion of the bungalow showing at the extreme left still shows its original construction, but all the other bungalows have now been re-developed, and previously vacant plots have been in-filled. Heavens Lane is named after Mr. Albert Heaven who owned most of the land at Redcliffe Bay in the 1920s and who was responsible for much of the development of the area between the two World Wars.

36. *Redcliffe Bay Estate – c. 1933.* Another view of the bungalows, originally built as weekend or holiday homes, but of which many became permanent homes, even though they had neither made-up roads nor modern conveniences such as electricity and running water. Just as people complain today about certain modern housing developments in Portishead, these bungalows also attracted criticism in the 1920s when one writer described them as 'a series of crimes'!

Junction of Hillside Road and Pembroke Road – 1988. Many bungalows were swept away during the large-scale re-development of Redcliffe Bay during the 1960s and 1970s, totally changing the character of the area as this view shows.

THE BEACH, REDCLIFF BAY, PORTISHEAD.

37. *Beach, Redcliffe Bay – c. 1935.* Like the Loaf Bathing Beach, Redcliffe Bay Beach was also extremely popular during the years between the Wars and had a café and changing cubicles. It was used both by the residents of the bungalows and also by day visitors to Portishead who came from Bristol by train and by bus. The beaches would be packed on summer weekends, and on Sunday evenings the queues for returning buses could be a couple of hundred yards long.

Beach, Redcliffe Bay – 1988. A Sunday afternoon and the beach is deserted. The beach café has gone and a number of modern properties in Hillside Road form the present-day skyline.

38. *Cricket field by Tower Farm, Down Road – c. 1960*. Tower Farm with its high stepped gables was an outstanding feature on the top of Portishead Down from the 1840s until the 1970s. Cricket was played nearby in the field alongside Down Road – one of the earliest references to the cricket field is in the '*Clevedon Mercury*' of 1887 when an athletic meeting was held there as part of Queen Victoria's Golden Jubilee celebrations. The home team in this match is the Portishead Optimists C.C., which was originally known as St. Peter's Church C.C.

Tower Farm Estate, Down Road – 1988. Tower Farm was demolished in the 1970s to make way for Tower Farm Estate, entered by Tower Road off Down Road. There are still a few of the old farm out-buildings at the end of Tower Road.